4

Ingredients

Christmas

Kim McCosker

4
Ingredients
Christmas

4 Ingredients
PO Box 400
Caloundra QLD 4551

ABN: 17 435 679 521

FB: facebook.com/4ingredientspage
YT: 4 Ingredients Channel
W: 4ingredients.com.au
T: @4ingredients

4 Ingredients Christmas

Photography: Megan Slade Photography: www.meganslade.com
Cover & Formatting: Tara Hale Illustration & Design: www.tarahale.com
Printing & Binding: Leo Paper Group, Hong Kong. Printed in China.
Australian Publisher: Simon & Schuster
New Zealand Publisher: Random House
UK Publisher: Simon & Schuster
USA Publisher: Atria Books (a division of Simon & Schuster)
ISBN: 978-1-84983-653-1

My intention with this cookbook was to create the
"Easiest entertaining cookbook you will ever own"

Easy Elegant Entertaining

with love

Kim

Abbreviations Used

Gram	g
Kilogram	kg
Millilitre	ml
Litre	ltr

Oven Temperature Guide

Making friends with your oven really helps when cooking.
Basically the Celsius temperature is about half the Fahrenheit temperature.

A lot of ovens these days offer the option to bake or fan bake (amongst others), as a rule, having the fan assisted option on will greatly increase the temperature in your oven and will shorten cooking times.

Our recipes have been compiled assuming a static conventional oven (non fan-forced) unless otherwise stated. If however your oven is fan forced as a general rule of thumb, conventional cooking temperatures are reduced by 20°C (this may vary between models). So if the recipe reads bake for 1 hour at 200°C that will be 1 hour at 180°C fan-forced.

Here's some help:

	Slow	Slow	Mod	Mod	Mod hot	Mod hot	Hot	Hot	Very hot
Fahrenheit	275	300	325	350	375	400	425	450	475
Celsius	140	150	165	180	190	200	220	230	240
Gas Mark	1	2	3	4	5	6	7	8	9

Guide to Weights & Measures

To help a recipe turn out right, you need to measure right. To make it easier all you need when cooking with 4 Ingredients are:

1 teaspoon:	1 tsp.
1 tablespoon:	1 tbs.
1 cup:	250ml

or the following:

Product	Grams per Cup
Almond meal	170
BBQ sauce	280
Butter	230
Basil Pesto	260
Breadcrumbs	130
Cheese	100
Chutney	300
Cornflakes	120
Cornflour	120
Desiccated coconut	120
Dried apricots	160
Dried mixed fruit	170
Flour – Plain	175
Flour – Self Raising	175
Honey	320
Icing sugar	120

Product	Grams per Cup
Jam	320
Maple syrup	240
Mayonnaise	260
Natural muesli	110
Nuts – Almonds	160
Nuts – Pecans	120
Nuts – Pine nuts	160
Nuts – Pistachios	120
Nuts – Walnuts	100
Pasta (dried)	75
Pasta sauce	175
Peanut butter	260
Popcorn	40
Polenta	100
Raisins	170
Rice	185

Product	Grams per Cup
Rice bubbles	80
Rolled oats	100
Salsa	175
Sour cream	320
Sultanas	170
Sugar – Brown	220
Sugar – Caster	200
Sugar – Raw	200
Sugar – White	220
Sweet chilli sauce	320
Tandoori paste	225
Tomato paste	260
Tomato sauce	280
Yoghurt	250

Table of Contents

With Thanks

As with all projects, they only see the light of day because of the help and contribution of others. These are my fabulous 'others' ...

Janelle McCosker: My assistant reasearcher and stylist who secretly harbours a desire to leave it all behind and start a career rapping "Nellie on ze Block!" ... Watch out JLO!

Melanie Roberts: What this lady can do with chocolate and candy is extraordinary.

Melinda Dines: Who ensured we were all fed and thirst-free and in her motherly way gathered props from Noosa to Neighbour.

Michelle Evans: Our link to the WORLD, life is simply 'funner' with this lady in it ... Is she Greek, Mexican, Italian, Kiwi? Who Cares; she's lovely!

Katie Guiver: The most eager taste tester amongst us.

Leonie Wolfsen: A calming, fun influence in any situation ... Can we have more of what she's having?

Jennette McCosker: Grandma, you are a fabulous ingredient in any gathering you add light and laughter ... Don't ever change!

Megan Slade: The Lady with the Lens ... Megs, no wonder you have been my photographer of choice for three years.

Glen Turnbull: Who (had we registered) could possibly own the record for most trips to a supermarket in a day ... You are a superstar husband!

You made such an almighty task, in such a short time, fun and exciting to be a part of ...

With Much Love & Gratitude

Kim

The Night Before Christmas

Magic Reindeer Dust

Makes 1

¼ cup (25g) oatmeal

2 tbs. sugar

1 tbs. glitter

In a small ziplock bag, or plastic gift bag, mix all ingredients together and tie with a ribbon. On Christmas Eve give to your children to ...

Sprinkle on the lawn at night

The moon will make it sparkle bright

As Santa's reindeer fly and roam

This will guide them to your home.

Reindeer Dip

Serves 8 Reindeers

5 medium carrots, peeled, sliced into 2cm pieces

250g pkt light cream cheese, softened

2 tbs. tahini

1 tbs. finely chopped fresh chives

Cook the carrots in a medium saucepan of boiling water for 10 minutes or until just tender. Drain and set aside for 10 minutes to cool slightly. Place the carrot and remaining ingredients in a blender and process until smooth. Season to taste. Transfer to a serving bowl. Cover with cling film and place in the fridge until ready to serve.

Reindeer Treats

Makes 16

250g matured cheese

125g butter

1 cup (175g) plain flour

Cayenne pepper

Mix all ingredients into a dough. Shape into a roll about 2cm thick. Wrap in baking paper and freeze for half an hour (or until firm enough to cut). Preheat oven to 180°C. Cut the roll into very thin (3mm) slices and bake until just golden brown.

Sprinkle on the lawn at night
The moon will make it sparkle bright
As Santa's reindeer fly and roam
This will guide them to your home

Brunch

Almond Bread

Makes **16** slices

4 egg whites
½ cup (100g) caster sugar
1 cup (175g) plain flour, sifted
250g whole almonds

Preheat oven to 180°C. Beat egg whites until stiff, gradually add sugar and beat for 2 minutes or until dissolved. Stir in flour and almonds. Place mixture in a paper-lined 23cm x 13cm loaf tin and bake for 40 minutes. Allow to completely cool. Using an electric knife, cut into thin slices. Place slices on a baking tray and return to a 130°C oven for 10–12 minutes or until golden and crisp.

Bacon & Avocado Bruschetta

SERVES 4

4 rindless bacon rashers
1 avocado
½ lemon
1 packet Bruschetta slices

In a frying pan cook bacon until nice and crisp. Meanwhile scoop the flesh of the avocado into a mixing bowl, add lemon juice and season, mix to combine. Toast bruschetta and spread a good tablespoon of mixture on each. Then top with crispy bacon, a squeeze of lemon and a twist of cracked pepper.

Breakfast Trifle

SERVES 8

4 cups (440g) muesli
12 strawberries, washed and quartered
½ sweet pineapple, chopped
500g Greek yoghurt

In eight cup-size glasses, layer the muesli, then fruit, then yoghurt
and repeat until full and top with a dollop of yoghurt.

Optional: *Garnish with a twig of something green
such as Strawberry Mint in this photo.*

Chocolate Crepes

Makes 24

2 eggs
1½ cups (375ml) milk
2¼ cups (280g) plain flour
Nutella to serve

Lightly whisk all ingredients (except Nutella) with 1½ cups (375ml) of water, careful not to overbeat, the batter should be quite thin. Heat a non-stick frying pan (add a little butter, to coat the base if needed). Pour a quarter cup of mixture into the pan and swirl in a circular motion outwards so the batter is even. Cook for 2 minutes or until the bottom is light brown. Flip to cook the other side for another minute. Remove and spread with the scrummy Nutella. Seal by folding the crepe in thirds, or roll and cut in half. Repeat until all the mixture is gone.

Croque Monsieur

16 slices sourdough
¼ cup (65g) Dijonnaise
250g sliced ham
2 cups (200g) grated Gruyere cheese

Spread 8 slices of bread with Dijonnaise. Then top with
ham and cheese and season before laying onto a sandwich press.
Top with another slice of bread and cook for 2–3 minutes each
side or until golden brown and the cheese melts.

Egg with Smoked Salmon Fingers

SERVES 8

8 eggs, soft boiled
6 slices dense bread such as sourdough, Turkish or brioche
1 tbs. (15g) butter
300g smoked salmon, cut into 2cm, long strips

Place the eggs in a small saucepan of water and bring to
the boil, boil for 6 minutes. Drain, and set aside for 10 minutes.
Preheat the grill to high. Cut the bread into long strips and arrange
on a grill rack. Cook for 1–2 minutes until toasted. Spread with a
little butter. Wrap strips of salmon around the lengths of the toast.
Place boiled eggs into egg cups and carefully slice off the
tops and serve with salmon 'fingers' to dip.

Grilled Fruit & Ricotta Stack

MAKES 4

2 pears
2 bananas
4 tbs. fresh ricotta
2 tbs. honey

Slice and grill the pears for 3 minutes. Layer pears and bananas. Top with ricotta and drizzle with honey.

Ham & Egg Quiches

MAKES 8

8 round slices of fresh ham
8 eggs
1 cup (100g) grated cheddar cheese
2 tbs. finely chopped parsley

Preheat oven to 180°C. Line eight large muffin cases with a round of ham. Beat together eggs and season with sea salt and cracked pepper. Divide the mixture evenly amongst the cases. Sprinkle each with cheese and parsley and bake for 20 minutes or until set.

Pancakes with Caramelised Bananas

SERVES 8

4 tbs. (60g) butter
¾ cup (165g) brown sugar
4 bananas, thickly sliced on the diagonal
16 pancakes

Place the butter and sugar in a small, non-stick frying pan.
Over medium heat stir to dissolve. Add bananas, reduce heat and
cook for 3 minutes or until the bananas have caramelised in the
mix. Heat the pancakes in the microwave for 30 seconds, stack
onto a serving plate and top with the divine toffee'd bananas.

Nibbles

Asparagus Wraps

MAKES APPROXIMATELY 16

2 bunches asparagus, ends trimmed
8 slices prosciutto
1 tbs. (15ml) extra virgin olive oil
1 tbs. (15ml) balsamic vinegar

Preheat oven to 180°C. Use a sharp knife to cut the prosciutto
lengthways into long, thin strips. Wrap a piece of prosciutto
around each asparagus spear, creating a long, spiral effect.
Place each spear on a paper-lined baking tray, drizzle with
oil and balsamic and season with sea salt and pepper.
Bake for 5 minutes. Serve immediately.

Baked Brie with Macadamia Praline

SERVES 8

¼ cup (55g) brown sugar
¼ cup (35g) raw macadamia nuts
1 tbs. (15ml) brandy
200g wheel of Brie

In a small bowl stir together the sugar, nuts, and brandy. Cover and chill for at least 2 hours. Preheat oven to 200°C. Place the Brie on an ovenproof platter and bake for 4 minutes or until the Brie is slightly softened. Spread the sugar mixture in an even layer on top of the warm Brie and bake for a further 3 minutes, or until the sugar melts ... This will become an 'entertaining' regular!

Optional: *Serve with wedges of freshly sliced apple and pear.*

Cheese Board

SERVES 8

250g creamy Brie
250g peppered cheddar
16 dates
250g seasonal grapes

A cheese board is a welcome indulgence at most gatherings. I will usually compliment a soft cheese with a hard cheese. As a rough guideline, allow a minimum of 50g of cheese per person when serving cheese at the start of a meal, and 100g at the end. Provide a variety of biscuits and/or breads as accompaniments to the cheese and some fresh fruit, grapes especially, to refresh the palette and compliment the cheese.

Hint: Never serve cheese straight from the fridge! Cold temperatures can make even the tastiest, ripest (and most expensive) cheeses taste bland; so make sure the cheese has at least 1 hour to find room temperature before it is served in order to fully appreciate both its aroma and flavour ... And as my Dad would say "Don't forget the port!"

Cucumber Ribbons & Prawns

Makes 12

12 cooked prawns
1 cucumber
2 tbs. sweet chilli sauce

Shell and devein prawns, leaving the tail intact, then rinse under cold running water. Trim ends from the cucumber and using a vegetable peeler, peel long, thin ribbons from cucumbers; discarding the seedy centres. Lay the prawns on a serving plate, snake the ribbon to form 3–4 rolls then lay atop the prawn. Skewer each and drizzle gently with sweet chilli sauce. Serve immediately on its own, or on the Tasting Plate featured on p.48.

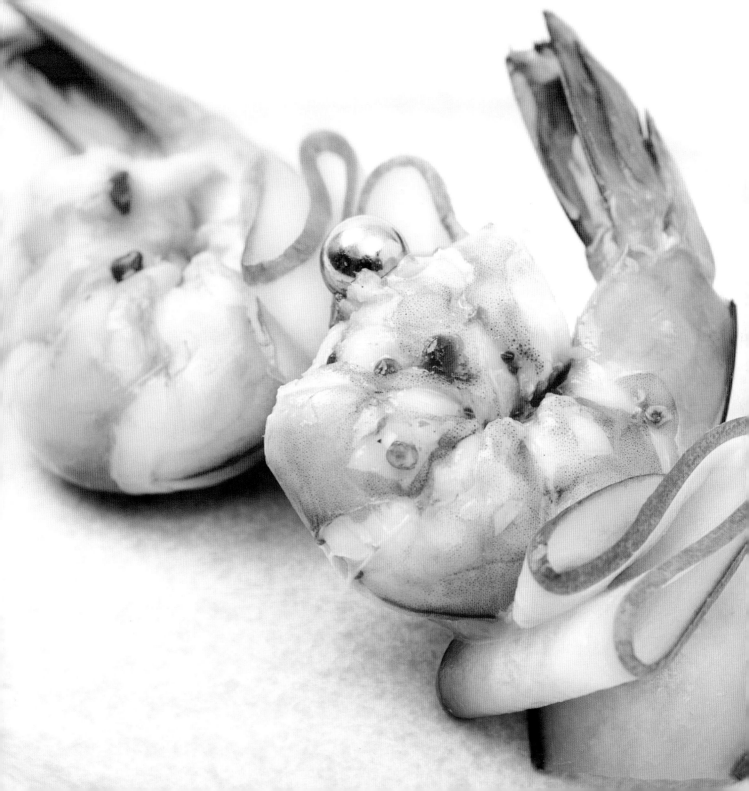

Decadent Salmon Stacks

500g pkt pumpernickel bread
250g light cream cheese
120g smoked salmon, finely chopped
120g roe

Line a 28cm x 13cm loaf tin with cling wrap. Trim the slices
of the bread so they fit the tin, then place aside. Pop cream
cheese and salmon in a bowl and season; beat until soft. Spread
approximately. ⅓ of the mixture over 3 slices of bread and turn
upside down in the prepared tin. Use remaining mixture to spread
evenly on the bread slices. Flip upside down and continue layers
until all ingredients are used. Cover with plastic and refrigerate for
2–3 hours. To serve, turn out onto a chopping board. Using a sharp
knife, cut into squares, top with roe and serve immediately.

Ricotta & Proscuitto Baked Pies

MAKES 12

5 slices prosciutto
400g fresh ricotta
6 sprigs fresh thyme, leaves picked
1 bunch chives, chopped

Preheat oven 180°C. Line the base and interior of each mini-muffin cup with the prosciutto. Combine ricotta, thyme and chives in a bowl and season. Distribute mixture evenly into muffin sections and bake for 15 minutes or until set. Remove tray and set aside for another 15 minutes to cool before serving.

Optional: *Bake topped with some halved cherry tomatoes.*

Skewer Duo

Chicken & Chorizo Skewers

Makes 8

1 chicken breast, cubed
1 chorizo sausage, sliced
Extra virgin olive oil spray
½ cup (90g) salsa

Onto a skewer thread meats. Spray lightly before grilling over a medium heat on a flat plate or barbeque for 4 minutes each side or until cooked through. Serve warm with salsa as a dipping sauce.

Heavenly Haloumi Skewers

Makes 8

24 basil large leaves
180g Haloumi cheese, cut into 16 cubes
16 semi dried tomatoes
3 tbs. (45g) balsamic glaze

Take four bamboo skewers and cut in half using good quality scissors. Thread each skewer with a basil leaf, followed by a slice of semi dried tomato, then a cube of haloumi and repeat until all 8 skewers are created. Preheat a flat plate or barbecue to medium. Place skewers onto barbecue and toast each side for 2 minutes or until golden. Serve warm seasoned with salt and pepper and drizzled with balsamic glaze.

Sweet Fig & Gorgonzola Pizza

SERVES 8

4 large flatbreads
6 figs, cut into quarters or eighths depending on their size
250g Gorgonzola, crumbled
4 tablespoons honey

Preheat oven to 170°C. On two paper-lined baking trays,
place the flatbreads and assemble each with figs and
gorgonzola before drizzling with honey. Season to taste.
Bake in the oven for 15 minutes or until golden in colour.
Once out of the oven, slice and serve immediately.

Optional: *Gorgonzola in this recipe can be substituted with*
a creamy blue cheese or even Brie.

Tasting Plate

Chicken & Port Paté

Serves 8

4 tbs. butter (60g) butter, softened
300g chicken livers, trimmed
2 spring onions, finely chopped
2 tbs. (30ml) port

Heat half the butter in a frying pan; cook livers, in batches until just browned. Add spring onions and cook, stirring until tender. Add port; cook, uncovered, until almost all of the liquid has evaporated. Blend or process the mixture until smooth. Blend again with remaining butter until smooth. Transfer to a bowl and refrigerate for at least 2 hours before serving.

Hint: This pate was my first foray into the world of homemade Pate and was extremely successful ... The Perfect Pate.

Watermelon & Feta Bites

Makes 24

½ seedless watermelon
24 mint leaves
2 tbs. (30ml) caramelised balsamic vinegar
200g feta cheese, cut into even cubes

Cut watermelon into 2cm cubes and place on a serving platter. Top with a cube of feta and a mint leaf. Spear all with a thin toothpick and lightly drizzle with caramelised balsamic vinegar.

Tip: If you don't have caramelised vinegar simply make your own: Pour ½ cup balsamic vinegar into a small frying pan and add 2 tbs. brown sugar. Over medium heat reduce until syrupy and allow to cool.

See page 38 for the Cucumber Ribbons & Prawn recipe.

Oyster Trios

SERVES 8–10

3 dozen natural oysters

BACON BALSAMIC & LEMON DRESSING

2 rashers rindless bacon, finely diced

2 tbs. (30ml) balsamic vinegar

Zest of ½ a lemon

In a small saucepan add the bacon and cook over medium heat until crisp. Stir in the balsamic vinegar and lemon rind and season. Allow to cool before serving on oysters.

GINGER WASABI MAYO

1 tbs. Gourmet Garden Ginger

⅓ cup (85g) whole egg mayonnaise

1 tsp. wasabi paste

1 tbs. finely chopped, pickled ginger

Place the first three ingredients into a bowl and stir until smooth. Spoon over oysters and sprinkle with pickled ginger.

OYSTERS MEXICANO

½ lime, juiced

¼ cup (55g) guacamole (or mashed avocado, seasoned)

12 corn chips

Pour lime evenly over each oyster. Spoon on guacamole, a little zest and stud with a corn chip to serve.

Entrées & Salads

An Entertainer's Timbale

SERVES 8

500g smoked chicken
250g seedless red grapes
3 ripe avocados
100g toasted pine nuts

Thinly slice the smoked chicken. Cut grapes in halves. Scoop
the flesh from your avocados and slice. Stack all of your
ingredients into a mould to make 8 petite salad timbales.
Top with toasted pine nuts, and gently remove the mould.
This dish can also be served as one large salad if you
are preparing more of a shared Christmas banquet.

Optional: *Drizzle with your favourite flavoured
oil or a squeeze of lemon juice.*

Hint: *A timbale is a dish of meat or fish cooked with other ingredients
in a pastry shell or in a mould. The moulds can be bought at any
kitchenwares shop and are really easy to use ... This recipe looks so
much more complicated than it was to prepare; easy entertaining.*

Carrot & Coriander Soup

SERVES 8

2 litres vegetable stock
2 onions, peeled and chopped
1 large bunch fresh coriander, chopped (leaves and roots)
12 carrots, peeled and roughly chopped

In a large saucepan, bring the vegetable stock to a warm temperature. Add onion, coriander leaves and roots, and carrots. Bring to the boil, reduce heat and simmer for 20 minutes or until the carrots are tender. Season with sea salt and pepper before blending. Serve garnished with a few coriander leaves.

Crispy Salmon Salad

SERVES 8

1½ kg fresh salmon fillet, cubed
500g fresh green beans, trimmed and blanched
350g marinated feta cheese, crumbled
1 bunch fresh dill, chopped

Using the oil from the feta, oil and heat a large frying pan,
add salmon cubes and sear on each side until crispy but still
pink in the centre (or cooked to your liking). In a large bowl
add and toss gently with remaining ingredients, taking care
not to break up the salmon.

Optional: This is also delicious drizzled with a little fresh lemon juice.

Garden Salad

SERVES 8

2 bunches asparagus, woody ends removed
4 rindless rashers bacon, halved
200g mixed salad leaves
¼ cup (125ml) caramelised balsamic vinegar

Into a large saucepan, add 3 cups (750ml) water and bring to the boil. Add asparagus and cook for 3 minutes. Combine cold water and ice cubes in a large bowl then remove the asparagus from the cooking pot and directly immerse in cold water. Drain excess water from the asparagus. Heat a non-stick frying pan and cook bacon for 4–5 minutes or until nice and crisp. Onto a large serving plate, sprinkle salad. Mix through asparagus and bacon. Season with sea salt and cracked black pepper. Drizzle with caramelised balsamic vinegar.

Optional: *For a festive effect, sprinkle with bright, vibrant nasturtiums just before serving.*

Mango, Avocado & Prawn Salad

Serves 4

2 large mangoes

2 avocados

12 cooked and peeled prawns

1 lime

Peel and slice the mangoes and avocados. Into individual glasses, layer the mango, avocado and prawns, ending with a lovely fresh prawn. Drizzle the juice from the cutting board over each and season. Chill, and when ready to serve garnish with a slice of lime.

Optional: A variation to this recipe is to add crispy bacon as a substitute for prawns. This is a stunning salad served in a glass bowl, lightly seasoned and tossed.

Prawns & Trio of Dipping Sauces

Place 500g freshly peeled prawns on a platter.
Serve with these easy to make sauces.

LEMONY AIOLI

½ cup (160g) whole-egg mayonnaise

1 clove garlic, crushed

2 tbs. (30g) lemon juice

½ tsp. lemon zest

In a medium bowl, mix all the ingredients together and season.

MANGO SALSA

1 cup mango flesh, cubed

1 lime

1 tbs. sweet chilli sauce

3 stems of fresh coriander, finely chopped

Cut the lime in half, juice and zest one half. Cut chilli in half, remove the seeds and chop very finely. Combine all ingredients adding sea salt and pepper to taste.

SWEET SOY SAUCE

2 tbs. soy sauce

2 tbs. honey

2 tbs. oyster sauce

Combine all ingredients in a bowl.

Rocket & Roquefort Soup

Serves 6-8

1.5 litres vegetable stock
300g rocket
250g Roquefort or other blue cheese
300ml cream

Into a large saucepan pour stock and bring almost to the boil.
Add the rocket and gently simmer for 4 minutes or until tender.
Crumble the cheese into the mix and simmer for 1 minute or until
the cheese has started to melt. Puree the soup in a blender, in
batches if necessary, until smooth. Stir in the cream and season
with cracked pepper. Ladle into warm bowls to serve.

Ruby Jewelled Seafood Salad

SERVES 8

1 large fennel bulb

2 pomegranates

8 bug tails, shelled and cleaned

4 oranges, peeled and segmented

Finely slice or shave fennel, discarding the harder green ends.
Collect the ruby seeds from the pomegranates by chopping them
open and scooping them out. Combine in a bowl with bug tails
and orange segments. Squeeze any remaining juice from
your oranges over the salad. Toss gently, season and serve.

Optional: Use lobster or prawn meat as a substitute to bugs!

Mains

Apple, Camembert & Potato Terrine

5 large potatoes, washed
3 green apples
150g butter
300g Camembert, chilled and very thinly sliced

Par boil potatoes in lightly salted water for about 15 minutes. Drain, cool then cut into slices 5mm thick. Heat half the butter in a frying pan and fry potato slices until just golden. Core and slice apples into 5mm slices. Preheat oven to 180°C. Line a terrine or baking dish with baking paper. Layer potato, apple and Camembert in the dish, seasoning as you go until all ingredients are used. With remaining butter grease a piece of foil and cover the terrine, sealing well. Place in a baking tray and half fill with boiling water. Bake for 20 minutes. Remove from baking dish, let it sit for 5–10 minutes, turn out and slice to serve hot with roast pork or chicken, or as a vegetarian main.

Citrus Glazed Ham

SERVES 8

5kg bone in, cured and smoked ham, skin on
4 oranges, cut into thin round slices
1 cup (320g) marmalade
½ cup (110g) brown sugar

Preheat oven 180°C and put the oven shelf to the lowest position. Peel the skin away from the ham using a sharp knife, leaving a thin layer of fat on the surface. Transfer the ham into a large roasting pan, or if too big onto a large baking tray. In a small saucepan over low heat cook the marmalade and sugar until combined. Glaze the ham. Arrange the orange slices, overlapping, on top. Secure each slice with a toothpick if needed. Brush with a little more glaze. Bake for 1 hour and 20 minutes. Brush occasionally with remaining glaze. Serve hot or cold.

Tip: *To remove rind use a small sharp knife to cut though rind. Cut along the shank and use your thumb to run underneath the skin to separate edges from fat. Starting from the widest edge, pulling rind from ham.*

Feta Stuffed Chicken Breast

SERVES 8

8 x 180g chicken breasts
100g semi dried tomatoes, chopped
200g feta, crumbled
¼ cup fresh tarragon

Preheat oven to 180°C. Using a long, thin knife cut a pocket in the thick part of the breast, careful not to cut through. Mix together tomatoes, feta and tarragon, fill pockets with mixture and secure with toothpicks. Rub the breasts with the oil from the semi dried tomatoes, season and place on a paper-lined baking tray. Bake for 30–35 minutes basting occasionally. Rest for 5 minutes before serving to the pleasure of your guests.

Guard of Honour

SERVES 8

16 lamb cutlets
1 tbs. (15ml) olive oil
4 tbs. dukkah
¼ cup (40g) pistachios, chopped

Preheat oven to 180°C. Trim excess fat from lamb and wrap
some aluminium foil 'crowns' around each bone to prevent
burning. Coat (or spray) lamb with olive oil, season with salt
and pepper. Seal lamb racks in a hot pan, remove and place
on baking tray, mix together dukkah and pistachios and press
firmly to coat the rack. Bake for 20–25 minutes, or to your liking.
Remove 'crowns' to serve.

Maple & Pepper Glazed Turkey

Serves 8

3 tbs. (45g) butter, melted

3 tbs. maple syrup

4kg turkey

¼ cup fresh sage leaves

Preheat oven to 200°C. Place the turkey on a large baking tray and using kitchen string tie together the back legs. Blend the butter and syrup and baste the entire turkey. Season generously with cracked pepper. Pour 1½ cups (375ml) water into the tray, and cover with foil. Pleat 3–4 sheets of alfoil together and tuck securely underneath, creating a sealed envelope around the turkey. Roast for 30 minutes, then reduce the heat to 180°C and continue to roast for 2 hours. As a general rule of thumb, for a turkey up to 5kg, allow 15 minutes per 500g, plus 10 minutes. 40 minutes beforehand, remove the alfoil and baste with juices in the pan. To serve, place the sage in a frying pan with 1 tsp. butter and gently fry until crisp; serve scattered across the turkey.

Tip: An easy check to see if your Turkey is cooked
is to insert a skewer into the thickest part of the thigh
— the juices should run clear.

Roast Pork & Crispy Crackling

SERVES 8

4kg leg of pork

3 tbs. (45ml) olive oil

2 tbs. salt flakes

1 lemon

Preheat oven to 220°C. Place the pork into a large baking dish, skin-side up. Using a sharp knife, score skin widthways at 1cm intervals, cutting deeply almost into the fat layer. Rub 2 tbs. oil onto the rind of the pork. Generously sprinkle salt flakes over rind and press into the scored skin. Drizzle remaining oil into the baking dish and bake for 20 minutes. Reduce heat to 180°C and cook for another 2 hours (or half hour per 500g).

Optional: *For a great crackling, look for a good coverage of fat and rind. Pork cuts that are suitable for roasting include leg, rack, rolled loin and rolled shoulder.*

Rosemary & Chicken Arrows

Makes 16

4 chicken breasts
16 long rosemary sprigs
2 tbs. honey
1 lemon, zest and juice

Cut each breast into 4 strips, gently mallet to tenderise
and place in a bowl. Remove the leaves from the rosemary
sprigs leaving a few at the top and soak the stems in cold water.
Chop removed leaves and add to the bowl with the honey,
lemon juice and zest and season with sea salt and pepper.
Cover and chill for at least 1 hour. Thread a piece of chicken onto
each rosemary arrow. Heat a grill and cook for 5–6 minutes,
turning occasionally, or until cooked through.

Salmon Terrine

Serves 8

500g sliced smoked salmon
450g chive and garlic cream cheese, softened
7g sachet gelatin
Juice of half a lemon, and wedges for garnish

Line a 23cm x 13cm loaf tin with baking paper overhanging the sides. Use approximately ¾ of the smoked salmon to line the tin, laying slices lengthwise across the base, up the sides and leaving enough overlap to fold over the top of the filling. Set aside enough of the smoked salmon to make a middle layer the length of the tin then chop the remaining salmon. Mix gelatin with 3 tbs. of hot water until dissolved. Beat the cream cheese, salmon, lemon juice and gelatin until well combined. Spoon half the mixture into the prepared tin. Lay the reserved smoked salmon slices on the mixture along the length of the tin, then spoon on the rest of the filling and smooth on top. Tap the tin on the work surface to expel any trapped air. Fold over the overhanging salmon slices to cover the top. Cover with plastic wrap and chill for a least 4 hours or overnight. To serve, turn out the terrine, then slice.

Sweet Pumpkin Galette

SERVES 8

2 sheets puff pastry, cut in half
1kg pumpkin, peeled, seeded, cut into 6cm pieces
1 cup (320g) sour cream
1 cup (320g) sweet chilli sauce

Preheat oven to 200°C. Place pumpkin wedges on a baking tray
and bake for 15 minutes. Remove from oven. Join two halves of
pastry together to create a long rectangular shape and roll in 1cm
of pastry to create a lip around the edges. Place each length on
a paper-lined baking tray. Spread sour cream over the bases.
Lay pumpkin on top, season with sea salt and cracked pepper
then drizzle with sweet chilli sauce. Place in oven and bake for
15 minutes or until the pastry edges are puffed and golden.

Hint: *Before baking, brush the pastry with beaten*
egg for a golden finish.

Salmon Ceviche

Serves 8

300g salmon fillet
1 red onion, thinly sliced rings
50g (small jar) capers, drained
1 lemon, peeled

Place the salmon fillet in the freezer for 10 minutes. Slice the salmon thinly and arrange on a serving plate, overlapping the slices slightly. Scatter over the onion, capers and thin slices of half the lemon. Season with sea salt and cracked black pepper and drizzle with the juice of the remaining lemon. Cover and refrigerate, leaving to marinate for 15 minutes.

Wild Mushroom Beef Wellington

SERVES 8

2 sheets puff pastry
1.5kg fillet beef
250g pepper pate
2 cups sliced mushrooms

Preheat oven to 180°C. Remove all fat from the meat. Tie the beef in four places so it holds its cylindrical shape while cooking. Season with sea salt and cracked pepper and sear all over, including the ends, in a hot, heavy-based non-stick frying pan for about 4 minutes. Place the meat on a baking tray and bake for 10 minutes. Remove and allow to become completely cold. In the same frying pan, add the sliced mushrooms and sauté for 6 minutes or until most of the liquid has evaporated. Season with salt and pepper and set aside to cool. Join the two sheets of puff pastry together, beat pate until soft and spread liberally over the pastry, leaving a 4cm border. Then top with seasoned mushrooms. Remove string from the fillet and place on top and wrap like a present, making sure it is totally encased. Decorate top with strips of pastry and bake in a 250°C oven for 5 minutes. Reduce heat to 180°C and bake for a further 40–45 minutes for a medium fillet.

Hint: Before baking, brush the pastry with beaten egg for a gorgeous golden finish.

Sauce & Gravy

CREAMY PEPPERCORN SAUCE

2 tbs. canned green peppercorns, rinsed and drained

½ cup (125ml) cream

⅓ cup (80ml) dry white wine

Place all ingredients into a small saucepan and gently bring to the boil, stirring regularly. Season with sea salt and pepper, reduce the heat and simmer for 10 minutes or until slightly reduced.

Optional: If serving this with a roast beef or Beef Wellington, use the pan juices to flavour the sauce too.

GLORIOUS GRAVY

¼ cup roast drippings (fat)

1 tablespoon plain flour

1 cup (250ml) stock

Salt

Place the roasting tin with drippings over a low flame, then using a wire whisk, stir in the flour and whisk until a light brown paste forms. Gradually pour in the stock, whisking all the time, until you have a thickened sauce. Season with sea salt and cracked pepper and simmer for 2 minutes, scraping any sticky bits from the sides of the pan (they are what contributes to a richly flavoured gravy).

A Plate of Asparagus

SERVES 8

800g asparagus, trimmed

Cook asparagus on a heated, oiled grill plate
for 5 minutes or until tender.

PARMESAN BUTTER

2 tbs. (30g) butter, melted

¼ cup (25g) shaved
Parmesan cheese

Combine in a small bowl and
serve drizzled over asparagus
with a sprinkle of salt flakes
and cracked pepper.

BALSAMIC SALSA

2 tbs. (30ml) olive oil

3 tsp. balsamic vinegar

1 (150g) tomato; peeled,
seeded, finely chopped

1 tbs. small, fresh basil leaves

Combine all ingredients in
a small bowl and gently
season. Serve over asparagus
spears.

TOASTED PINE NUTS

3 tablespoons pine nuts

1 tbs. (30ml) olive oil

1 teaspoon fresh lemon juice

In a small frying pan add
olive oil and lemon juice,
over medium heat, sauté
pine nuts for 2–3 minutes or
until browned. Serve over
asparagus spears.

Beans with Garlic, Lemony Butter

SERVES 8

3 tbs. (45g) butter, softened
1 lemon, finely zested
1 clove garlic
400g beans, topped

Put the butter, zest and garlic in a medium bowl and stir until
well combined. Season and chill in the refrigerator. Meanwhile,
bring a saucepan of water to the boil, add a pinch of salt and beans
and cook for 2–3 minutes or until just tender. Drain and transfer
to a serving dish. Dollop with butter. Toss and serve.

*Optional: For presentation, wrap equal amounts
of beans with a cucumber ribbon.*

Golden Roast Potatoes

Serves 8

1.5kg potatoes (King Edward, Desiree, Kipfler)
¼ cup (60ml) olive oil
16 cloves garlic, skin on
Zest from one lemon

Wash potatoes and pop them in a saucepan large enough to hold them in a single layer. Add the salt and enough water to just cover. Bring to the boil; cover and reduce heat. Simmer for 20 minutes or until tender when tested with a skewer. Drain and return to the saucepan. Place over medium heat for 2 minutes to dry the potatoes. Add the oil to a large roasting pan and place in the oven for 2 minutes or until really hot. Squash the potatoes gently with a potato masher so that they burst skins. Remove the roasting pan and add the potatoes and garlic cloves. Roll to coat in the oil. Roast, turning occasionally, for 45 minutes or until crispy. Remove the potatoes and garlic, drain of excess oil, season and serve scattered with the zest.

Honey Glazed Sweet Potato

SERVES 8

2.5kg sweet potato
¾ cup (240g) honey
2 tbs. freshly chopped rosemary

Preheat oven 200°C. Peel the sweet potatoes and cut into
equal size pieces, approximately 4cm long. Combine honey and
rosemary in a large bowl, add sweet potato, season and toss
to coat. Place onto a paper-lined baking tray and roast for
25 minutes or until tender and caramelised.

Seasoned Roast Vegetables

SERVES 8

8 slender carrots, peeled
4 large parsnips, peeled and cut in half or quarters
2 beetroots, peeled and cut into thick wedges
½ cup (125ml) olive oil

Preheat the oven to 180°C. Put the vegetables in a large baking dish. Season well with sea salt and cracked pepper, drizzle generously with olive oil, toss them to coat evenly. Bake, stirring the vegetables occasionally, for 45 minutes or until tender and golden brown. Transfer to a platter to accompany a roasted main course.

Dessert

A Garden Bed Pavlova

5 egg whites
1¼ cups (250g) caster sugar
1 tbs. cornflour
Edible flowers; Petunias and nasturtiums

Preheat oven to 130°C. Line a large baking tray with baking paper. Beat the egg whites in a large bowl with an electric mixer until soft peaks form. Gradually add the sugar, beating until dissolved between additions, scraping down the side of the bowl occasionally. Use a large spatula to fold in the cornflour. Pile the meringue into the centre of the prepared tray, then with the spatula, spread the meringue into a 23cm circle, making a shallow well in the centre. Reduce the oven temperature to 100°C and bake in the lower half of the oven for 1½ hours or until dry and crisp. Turn off the oven and cool the pavlova in the oven with its door ajar. Serve topped with whipped cream and randomly scattered edible flowers.

Hint: Not all flowers are edible, but here are those that are; lavender, thyme, dill, coriander, day lily, zucchini flowers, Nasturtiums, chives, and basil. In addition I candied one of our neighbours rose petals, by washing with egg whites and dusting with caster sugar, I did this a day ahead of time to allow time for setting.

Caramel Ice-Cream

SERVES 8

300ml cream
395g tin Carnation Caramel or Top 'n' Fill, beaten

Whip the cream until peaks are just starting to form.
Mix in the caramel until well combined. Transfer into
a paper-lined 23cm x 13cm loaf tin and freeze overnight.

Chocolate Tofu Mousse

SERVES 4

340g pkt silken tofu, room temperature
280g dark chocolate
2 tbs. pure maple syrup
1 tsp. vanilla extract

Blend the tofu in a blender, or with a hand held mixer until just smooth. In a microwave dish, melt chocolate, stirring every 30 seconds until nice and smooth. Add maple syrup and vanilla to the melted chocolate and stir to combine. Add tofu and mix until creamy. Pour or scrape into four small serving dishes, or long tall champagne flutes. Chill until set.

Optional: *When entertaining I garnish with long shards of chocolate and a dollop of whipped cream for an impressive finish.*

Christmas Cake

1kg dried mixed fruit
3 cups (750ml) fruit juice
3 cups (525g) self raising flour

Soak fruits in juice overnight. Preheat oven to 125°C. Stir flour into soaked fruit and mix well. Spoon mixture into a 22cm lined cake tin. Bake for 2½ hours in the bottom of the oven or until cooked through. Remove and leave to cool. Wrap in alfoil or place in an air tight container where this cake will keep nicely for 3–4 weeks.

Optional: Add a shot of your favourite tipple, sherry, brandy, rum or Grand Marnier.

Serving Suggestion: Decorate as you wish; cherries, nuts, ginger or as I have done with a rich chocolate ganache, by warming a cup of cream and adding a 250g block of dark chocolate to it.

Christmas Cake Ice-Cream Terrine

SERVES 8

500g Christmas cake, cut into 1½cm slices
3 tbs. (45ml) Cointreau
1 tbs. finely grated orange rind
2 litres vanilla ice-cream, softened

Line a 23cm x 13cm loaf tin with cling wrap. Brush cake slices with Cointreau. Stir rind into softened ice-cream. Spread half the ice-cream mixture into the tin; top with cake slices then remaining ice-cream. Cover completely with plastic wrap and freeze overnight. When ready to serve, use a hot knife to cut the terrine into eight delicious slices.

Fruit Mince Meringue Tarts

MAKES 24

1 cup (200g) caster sugar
2 egg whites
500g jar fruit mince
2 sheets shortcrust pastry

Preheat oven to 180°C. Roll the pastry out onto a clean, flat surface and using a round scone cutter with scalloped edging cut 24 x 8cm rounds. Gently line 2 x 12 cup patty cake tins with the rounds and bake for 5 minutes. Fill the pre-baked pastry cases with 1 tablespoon of fruit mince. Combine sugar and ¼ cup (60ml) of water in a small saucepan. Stir on low heat until sugar dissolves. Increase heat to medium. Simmer for 3–4 minutes or until the syrup reaches soft-ball stage (to test, drop a teaspoonful of syrup into a small bowl of water — the syrup should form a ball). Meanwhile, using an electric mixer, beat egg whites until firm peaks form. As soon as the syrup is ready, add to meringue in a slow, steady stream, beating constantly on medium speed, until thick and glossy. Pipe or spoon meringue over tarts. Place tarts on a baking tray and bake for 5 minutes, or until golden. Serve warm or at room temperature.

Optional: Cut star shapes from remaining pastry and put on alternate tarts. Brush with a beaten egg and sprinkle with demerara sugar. Bake at 180°C for 15–20 minutes.

Plum Pudding

Serves 12

2 cups (350g) self raising flour
1 cup (220g) caster sugar
1 kg pkt dried mixed fruit
1 tbs. bicarbonate of soda

Mix the first three ingredients together in a large bowl.
Then mix 2 cups (500ml) of boiling water with bicarbonate
of soda, add to the mixture and mix through with a knife. Cover
and leave overnight. Mix well the next morning. Place in a damp
floured cloth and tie very securely. Boil in a large saucepan for
3 hours ensuring it does not come off the boil, or boil dry.
Remove and cool slightly before carefully peeling the cloth
so as not to disrupt the delicious, thick skin that forms.

Custard

Brandy Custard

Serves 4

2 cups (500ml) milk
6 egg yolks
½ cup (100g) caster sugar
1 tbs. brandy

Place the milk in a large saucepan and bring to a simmer over medium/high heat. Remove from heat and set aside. Whisk together the eggs yolks and sugar in a heatproof bowl. Gradually stir in the warm milk. Pour the liquid into the saucepan and place over low heat. Cook, stirring constantly for 10 minutes or until custard coats the back of the spoon. Add the brandy and stir to combine.

Optional: Add half a teaspoon of vanilla essence to the eggs if in your pantry.

Hint: Can I suggest seeing that you have soooo many eggs whites now, you might like to try our Garden Bed Pavlova recipe p.108.

Creamy Custard

Serves 4

½ cup (110g) caster sugar
1 cup (250ml) water
4 egg yolks
300ml thickened cream, lightly whipped

Combine sugar and the water in small saucepan; stir over medium heat, without boiling, until sugar is dissolved. Bring to the boil; simmer, uncovered, without stirring, until sugar syrup is reduced to about ½ cup (125ml). Beat egg yolks in small bowl with electric mixed until thick and creamy. Gradually beat in hot sugar syrup in a thin stream; beat until mixture is thick and creamy. Fold in cream. Refrigerate until ready to serve.

Roly-Poly Trifle

500g Swiss roll
2 cups whipped cream
7g sachet gelatin
2 punnets strawberries, 1½ chopped, the rest to decorate

Line a deep round bowl (so that if turned upside down it is a dome shape) with glad wrap. Slice jam roll into 1cm thick slices and line the entire bowl with them. Whip cream just until stiff peaks form. Dissolve gelatine in 3 tbs. of warm water, stirring vigorously until dissolved then add to the cream. Stir in sliced strawberries. Pour the strawberry cream mixture over the cake slices in the bowl. Set in the fridge for at least 3–4 hours. When set, carefully turn upside down onto a serving plate. Decorate with strawberries and serve.

Rum & Raisin Decadence

SERVES 8

A BEAUTIFUL RECIPE FROM MARIE McCOLL.

1 cup (170g) raisins
½ cup (125ml) dark rum
2 litres choc-chip ice-cream, softened
250g choc-coated macadamias, cut in half

Soak the raisins in the rum for at least 2–3 hours. Whip the
ice-cream until peaks are just starting to form. Place the
ice-cream in a large bowl, fold in the raisin mixture and two-thirds
of the macadamias. Scrape the mixture into a baking paper-lined
23cm x 13cm loaf tin. Cover with cling wrap and freeze overnight.
When ready to serve turn out onto a chilled serving plate and
top with the extra nuts.

White Christmas Cheesecake

SERVES 8

250g cream cheese, softened
400g can condensed milk
7g sachet gelatine
150g white chocolate

In medium bowl, beat cream cheese until smooth. Add condensed milk and continue beating until well combined. Dissolve gelatine in 3 tbs. of warm water, stirring vigorously. Add to the mixture. Pour into a base of choice and chill for at least 4 hours prior to serving. With 30 minutes remaining, melt the chocolate in a clean, dry microwave dish stirring every 30 seconds until nice and smooth. Pour chocolate onto a paper-lined baking tray and spread it out evenly. Refrigerate for 15 minutes. Remove and with a sharp knife cut long, thin shards from the chocolate, enough to completely cover the top of the cheesecake.

Optional: *There are a number of really easy base recipes available; store bought, short crust pastry, vanilla cake mix with butter, sweet biscuits crushed with butter and so on ... Choose whichever you prefer for this fabulous filling.*

Sweet Treats

A Box of Chocolates

MAKES 30

2 x 150g pkt Oreo biscuits
125g cream cheese, softened
150g milk chocolate

In a food processor, blend cookies to a fine meal. Pour into
a large bowl and add cream cheese, mixing together until there
are no traces of white. Remove mixture and roll into balls, place
on a paper-lined baking tray and refrigerate for 30 minutes. Melt
chocolate in a microwave safe dish on medium high stirring every
30 seconds until nice and smooth. Add a chilled ball one at a time
and coat in the chocolate. Place back onto the tray, when all the
balls are done, refrigerate to set.

*Optional Coatings: When ready to serve, remove these terrific
truffles from the fridge and sit for 10 minutes so they begin
to sweat. This makes it easier for selected coatings to stick.
Here are the various options we used:*

*• Dessicated coconut • Crushed nuts • Crushed pistachios
• Cocoa powder • White chocolate • Edible glitter
• Jelly crystals • Salt Flakes*

Angel Wings

MAKES 24

200g white chocolate
24 plump, dried apricots
½ cup (80g) pistachios, finely chopped

In a microwave safe bowl, place chocolate pieces and melt on medium-high, stirring every 30 seconds until nice and smooth. Take an apricot one at a time and dip it into the melted chocolate, covering only half, then dip the chocolate end into the pistachios. Place on a paper-lined baking tray and refrigerate for 10 minutes or until set. Pop in a jar or container and keep refrigerated.

Cherry Baubles

MAKES 24

150g milk chocolate
24 plump, ripe cherries, stalks intact

In a microwave safe bowl, place chocolate pieces and melt on medium-high, stirring every 30 seconds until nice and smooth. Line a baking tray with baking paper. Take a cherry, one at a time, and dip half way into the melted chocolate, then place on the prepared tray. Repeat until all cherries are covered. Chill until ready to serve.

Chocolate Coated Orange Candy

SERVES 8

4 oranges
3 cups (600g) caster sugar
1 cup (250ml) water
250g dark chocolate

Slice the orange peel into ½cm strips leaving pith on. Place the peel in a pot of water and bring to the boil, strain and repeat process once more. Add peel back, this time with water and sugar. Simmer for 40 minutes, remove from syrup and dry on a wire rack. In a microwave dish, place chocolate and melt on medium-high heat stirring every 30 seconds until smooth. Dip each piece of orange candy in chocolate three-quarters the length and place prepared baking tray to set.

Optional: *Make sure you utilize the remainder of your orange for fresh juice or in our Ruby Jewelled Seafood Salad on p.68.*

Choc Cherry Fudge

250g dark chocolate
400g can condensed milk
1 cup (120g) walnuts, chopped
16 marachino cherries, stalks on

In a large microwave-safe bowl, melt chocolate and condensed milk on medium-high for 4 minutes, checking at regular intervals. Stir vigorously to combine then add the nuts. Spread in a 16cm x 16cm baking tray lined with baking paper. Lightly draw lines on the lid, first in half, then quarters, eights and finally sixteenths and into the centre of each gently press a pretty red cherry. Refrigerate to set. Remove and cut along lines to serve.

Christmas Glitter Pops

MAKES 24

500g moist Christmas cake or heavy fruit cake
½ cup (125ml) dark rum
350g white chocolate
Edible glitter

Place Christmas cake and rum in a food processor and blend until combined. Refrigerate for 30 minutes. Line a baking tray with baking paper. Using a teaspoon, take a generous amount of mixture and roll into balls. Melt the chocolate in a clean, dry microwave dish stirring every 30 seconds until creamy. Roll each ball into chocolate and place onto the prepared tray. When complete, chill for 15 minutes or until set. Just before serving, remove from fridge, gently pierce with a cake pop and sit for 10 minutes to sweat. Roll thoroughly in edible glitter before serving to the delight of all.

Cinnamon Stars

MAKES 24

2 egg whites
2¼ cups (270g) icing sugar, sifted
1½ cups (250g) ground almonds
1½ tablespoons ground cinnamon

Beat the egg whites lightly with a wooden spoon in a large bowl. Gradually stir in the icing sugar to form a smooth paste. Remove ⅓ cup, cover and set aside. Add the almonds and cinnamon to the remaining icing and gently press together with your hands. Add 1 teaspoon water if the mixture is too dry. Press together well before adding any water as the warmth of your hands will soften the mixture. Lightly dust a work surface with icing sugar and roll out the mixture to about 3mm thick. Spread with a thin layer of the reserved icing. Leave, uncovered, at room temperature for 30–35 minutes, or until the icing has set. Preheat the oven to 150°C. Cut out shapes using a variety of star cutters. Dip the cutters in icing sugar to help prevent sticking. Place the stars on a paper-lined baking tray and cook for 10 minutes, or until just firm. Cool on the tray. Store in an airtight container.

Coconut Cream Truffles

Makes 24

⅓ cup (125ml) coconut cream
1 cup (120g) shredded coconut
220g white chocolate, chopped
1 tbs. (15g) butter

In a medium size saucepan, heat cream and ¾ cup of coconut to a simmer. Remove from heat and stir in chocolate. Let mixture sit for about 5 minutes. Add butter and stir to combine all the ingredients. Cover and chill for 3 hours. Roll the mixture with a teaspoon into balls and then in the remaining coconut to coat. Place on a paper-lined baking tray, cover and chill for at least 2 hours before serving.

Hint: *These make a thoughtful gift packaged in a clear box, or in cellophane for any occasion.*

Lime & Macadamia Fudge

Makes 24

400g can condensed milk
500g white chocolate
150g macadamia nuts, chopped
2 limes, zest finely grated

Line an 18cm square tin with baking paper. Place condensed milk and chocolate pieces in a saucepan and stir over a low heat until smooth then remove from heat. Add nuts and zest and mix well. Pour into tin and refrigerate overnight prior to cutting.

Marzipan Marbles

MAKES 40

500g almond icing, softened
4 cups (500g) icing sugar
100ml light corn syrup
40 pecan halves

Place half the almond icing and icing sugar in a blender
and blend until combined. Add half the corn syrup and
continue to blend until well combined. Turn out onto a flat surface.
Repeat with remaining ingredients and blend until combined.
Knead both lots of mixture until a smooth dough forms. Line
a baking tray with baking paper. Roll tablespoons of the mixture
into balls and pop onto the tray. Firmly press a pecan into the
centre of each round. Set aside for 4 hours or until firm.

Hint: Light corn syrup is found in most supermarkets.

Peppermint Crème Checkers

Makes 24

250g dark chocolate
250g white chocolate
250g Peppermint Crème biscuits
125g cream cheese, softened

In a separate microwave-safe dish, melt the dark chocolate on a medium-high heat stirring every 30 seconds until silky smooth. Into a 12-hole square chocolate mould (or an ice-cube tray) spoon enough chocolate to cover the base. Refrigerate to set. Repeat the process with the white chocolate. Meanwhile, process the biscuits in a blender until a fine meal results. Add softened cream cheese and blend until well combined. Remove chocolate moulds and using a teaspoon roll a ball of mixture and pop onto the chocolate base. Lightly press to spread almost to the edges. Spoon remaining chocolate in, covering the filling. Refrigerate for half an hour or until set.

Optional: These are equally delicious, and easier if you don't have a square chocolate mould, rolled into balls, then dipped in chocolate to coat.

Reindeer Bark

50g peppermint candy canes
200g dark chocolate

Break canes into pieces and place in a plastic bag. Squeeze bag to expel air. Wrap the bag in a tea towel, place on a hard surface and pound with a rolling pin until the canes are crushed. In a microwave safe dish, melt the chocolate on medium-high stirring every 30 seconds until silky smooth. Pour the chocolate onto a paper-lined baking tray, about 2mm thick. Sprinkle with crushed cane. Sit aside for 20 minutes, or in the fridge if room temperature is too warm, until set. Break into pieces to serve.

Hint: Store bark in an airtight container in a cool place for up to 5 days.

Rocky Road Bon Bons

MAKES 16

250g chocolate; dark, milk or white
100g macadamia nuts, roughly chopped
1 cup marshmallows, cut in half
150g Turkish delight, roughly chopped

Break chocolate into pieces and melt in a microwave safe dish on medium-high heat stirring every 30 seconds. Allow to cool slightly before adding remaining ingredients. Mix until well combined. Line a 9cm x 13cm loaf tin with baking paper, pour the mixture into it, neaten edges and refrigerate until set. Remove and cut into 8 rectangular slices. Cut in half again and wrap each in clear cellophane. These make a beautiful handmade Christmas gift tied at each end with a pretty ribbon.

Salted Caramel Charms

MAKES 24

⅓ cup (75g) caster sugar
⅔ cup (160ml) cream
200g dark chocolate, chopped coarsely
200g milk chocolate

Place sugar with 2 tbs. water in a small saucepan, over medium heat, stir until it dissolves. Bring to the boil, when golden brown, add the cream, stir over a low heat until toffee pieces melt. Remove from heat, stir in dark chocolate and ½ tsp. salt flakes. Quickly roll the mixture into teaspoon size balls, place on a paper-lined baking tray and freeze for 30 minutes. With 5 minutes to go, place milk chocolate in a large microwave safe bowl and melt on high, stirring every 20 seconds until smooth. Using two spoons, dip truffles into milk chocolate and return to the tray. Top each truffle with a sprinkle of 4–5 coarse salt flakes. Refrigerate to set.

Drinks

Christmas Candy Martini

Makes 1

60ml Vanilla Vodka
30ml White Chocolate Liqueur
30ml Peppermint Schnapps
1 teaspoon of Grenadine

Fill a martini shaker with ice. Add vodka, liqueur and schnapps. Shake and strain into a chilled martini glass. Add a teaspoon of Grenadine slowly down the edge of the glass, it will sink to the bottom forming a gloriously coloured base.

Festive Fruit Fizz

SERVES 8

1 cup watermelon, cut into cubes
10 strawberries, hulled and halved
1 cup fresh, sweet pineapple cubes
1 litre Lemonade (or sparkling mineral water)

Put cubes of watermelon, strawberries and a pineapple pieces on a baking tray and freeze for several hours or until frozen. Process the frozen fruit in a blender until smooth. Spoon blended fruit mixture into a pitcher, add icy cold lemonade or sparkling mineral water and serve.

Tipsy Tip: *Add a little vodka for the adults.*

Mango Daiquiri

Makes 1

1 mango, peeled and chopped
30ml STROM
1 cup ice
1 lime

Place all ingredients into a blender including the juice of one lime and blend until nice and smooth. Use the lime rind to garnish.

Optional: *For a thicker consistency use frozen mango and in lieu of STROM Spirits, a fine brandy works just as well.*

Mint Tea

SERVES 4

20 fresh mint leaves
1 litre boiling water

Place the leaves into a tea infuser or a tea strainer. Pour over the water and steep for about 3–4 minutes. Drink and enjoy!

Watermelon Bellini

Makes 8

3 cups cubed watermelon, chilled
2 limes
1 cup (250ml) cloudy apple juice
1 litre chilled dry, light champagne

Place watermelon, 2 tablespoons of lime juice and the cloudy apple juice in a blender; process until smooth. Pour about ½ cup watermelon mixture into 8 champagne flutes and top with champagne. Garnish each with Julienne-cut lime rind to decorate. Serve immediately.

Invitation

Join our Foodie Family

At 4 ingredients we cultivate a family of busy people all bound together by the desire to create good, healthy, homemade meals quickly, easily and economically.

Our aim is to save us all precious time and money in the kitchen. If this is you too, then we invite you to join our growing family where we share kitchen wisdom daily.

If you have a favourite recipe, or a tip that has worked for you in your kitchen and think others would enjoy it, please join our family at:

 facebook.com/4ingredientspage

 4 Ingredients Channel

 4ingredients.com.au

 @4ingredients

Happy Entertaining!

Kim

Bibliography

BOOKS

McCosker, Kim: Bermingham, Rachael. **4 Ingredients.** Simon and Schuster Australia Pty Ltd. Suite19A / Level 1 / 450–476 Miller St Cammeray NSW 2062 Australia; 2007.

McCosker, Kim: Bermingham, Rachael. **4 Ingredients 2.** Simon & Schuster Australia Pty Ltd. Suite19A / Level 1 / 450–476 Miller St Cammeray NSW 2062 Australia; 2008.

McCosker, Kim: Bermingham, Rachael. **4 Ingredients Fast Fresh & Healthy.** Hay House 18/36 Ralph St, Alexandria NSW 2015 Australia; 2010.

Gorgeous Christmas. Annie Bell. Kyle Cathie Ltd. 122 Arlington Road. London NW17HP

Christmas December 2010. **Australian Women's Weekly Magazine.** ACP Magazines Ltd.54–58 Park St. Sydney NSW 2000.

WEBPAGES

Easy Dinner Party Entertaining http://www.myrecipes.com/menus/easy-dinner-party-entertaining

British Cheese Boards http://www.gourmet-food.com/gourmet-cheese-assortment/english-cheese-board

Christmas Fare http://www.cooks.com/rec/search/0,1-0,christmas

Chocolate Ganache http://allrecipes.com/Recipe/chocolate-ganache

Roasted Vegetables http://allrecipes.com/Recipe/roasted vegetables

Candied Orange http://www.foodnetwork.com/recipes/food-network-kitchens/candied-orange-recipe

Marzipan Australia http://www.marzipanaustralia.com.au/marzipan-dessert.asp

STROM Spirit http://www.stromspirits.com

Index